A Witch's Prayerbook

Edited by Teresa Sareta

by

JoAnne Spiese

THG StarDragon Publishing

Copyrights

Copyright © 2015 by Jo Anne Spiese
Cover art by Teresa Garcia and Marantha D. Jennelle
Interior art by Marantha D. Jennelle

All rights reserved. This book or any portion thereof may not be reproduced or used in any manner whatsoever without the express written permission of the publisher except for the use of brief quotations in a book review. All of these poems were written by the author in the periods between 2010 and 2015, some of which have appeared elsewhere.

Printed in the United States of America

First Printing, 2015
LCCN: 2014952032

ISBN-13: 978-1502450944
ISBN-10: 1502450941

THG StarDragon Publishing
PO Box 249
McCloud, CA 96057
USA

www.thgstardragon.com

Contents

Introduction	1
Fate and Love	5
Seasonal and Lunar	27
Natural Forces, Prayers & Devotions	59
Spirits	83
Light	93
Cycles Onward	103
Glossary	117
About the Poetess	119

Dedicated to all those who have gone before me.

I want to thank my publisher and editor Teresa Garcia. She showed me faith and understanding. Both of which are so very important in life.

Editor's Note

This book is not recommended for minors due to the sexual content of some of the poems and prayers. In this faith the union of male and female is considered sacred and an expression of the divine, thus a vehicle to become one with All That Is. If you are uncomfortable with such a subject or are triggered by such then I suggest skipping the first few poems within "Fate and Love." Or you could sit with those and use the opportunity to examine what you feel is right for you and why, and write your own prayer-poems exploring the subject of union within your comfort zone.

Although this book is primarily from the feminine view of the Witches' faith and focuses a great deal on the female and the Goddess, please remember the males in the faith and the various faces of the God. Not every witch, male or female, is equally comfortable with both sides of the Sacred. As one that for a long time was uncomfortable with the male side of the sacred, I can vouch on how it is a long road, although I have become equally comfortable. Perhaps, somewhere out there, is a male of this faith that would like to pick up the pen to write a book of masculine prayers exploring all aspects of the God to answer this book with strength and support.

I have endeavored to flow the poems together in a way so as to tell a story in addition to being the prayerbook that I was originally approached to publish. Thus we start at the beginning. There is more than one way to pray, and a good deal of these poems are in thanks, not always "asking for something." Also, in the nature of a story and cycles, it must be remembered that the end is only the beginning. I encourage all readers to feel free to use Ms. Spiese's prayers as a springboard for reaching their own dreams.

It is never too late.

Teresa Garcia
2015

Introduction:

As the sun dawned on man
We were there.

As the moon rose and the stars shone
We were there.

As gatherers became hunters
We were there.

We praised what was seen and drew the unknown to ourselves.
We protected the clan and sought safety for our people.
We gave strength for the hunt and drew prey to the hunters.
We danced under the full moon.
We praised the Goddess and Gods.
We gave aid with our skills and herbs.
We cured the ill and comforted the dying.
We assisted in the renewal of life through birth.
We were the wise women, the elders.
We led our clan.
We were the first Witches.

Time changed and our role evolved, we became the guardians of the Goddess and Gods. We served the men who controlled our society. We maintained the temples of the Goddess and served her with our lives. We were the priestesses. We served our people. We dedicated our lives to the Goddess. We were called on to serve our people with our wisdom. Our hearts were bound to our past. We were bound to our Siblings. We were Witches.

The world had changed and expanded. Societies clashed with each other. Blood was spilled in the name of the one God.

We remained.

We passed our knowledge to our sisters and daughters. We danced under the full moon and praised the Goddess. But there was change in the wind. Our roles were diminished. The Goddess, Our Mother Earth had been replaced. One God, the Goddess had been replaced. But we remained.

The followers of this one God would slay all that did not believe as they did. Civilizations fell, destroyed for their beliefs. Our temples ran red with their blood. They took our power and put us in chains that would last for hundreds of years.

We hid. They found us. We were dragged before them. Threatened, tortured, jailed, abused, hung and burned, thousands of women, children, and men were killed. What did we die for? A single fearful word... "*Witch.*" Innocent blood stained the hands of the righteous and God fearing clergy. Mass hysteria engulfed the world. "Witch, Witch, you're a Witch" was their chant. Their words brought fear to the very depth of our souls.

We survived.

We have come out of the broom closet. We stand tall in the sunlight and praise the Goddess. We are descendants of the first Witches that danced under the full moon and praised what they saw.

I walk a path of those who have gone before me.
My life is full.
I know my power.
My life serves my Goddess.

My strength comes each day from the Goddess. I have chosen her before all, for she has shown herself to me. I am dedicated to her. For I have been her daughter throughout the ages. I stand with my Sisters and Brothers. I have learned from those who have passed before me, for I am Witch.

I remain, and so shall you.

Show Yourself

The time has come to show yourself.

No longer can you hide in the shadows,
Darkness will not cover who you are.
Stillness is not an enemy.

Release your fear.
Embrace the unknown.
Find those who also hide.
Be strong in your will.

Stand tall before the accuser.
Drop your cloak,
Come into the light.

Reach for your Sisters and Brothers,
Take their hands and come forth.
Know who you are.

Feel the warmth.
Let love surround you.
Unearth your power.
Discover your roots.
See your path.

Go forth in safety.

The new Moon is yours.
She calls to us.
Her call is to you.
Walk knowing your authority.
Watch your control grow.

Discover yourself.
Be who you are born to be.
Uncover the Secrets.
Be in command of all you survey.

Listen to the wind.
Feel the coolness of the rain.
Touch the earth.
Watch the fire grow,
You are one among us.

Come, join your siblings.

Take to your broom.
Fly high into the night.
Catch the moon.
Know who you are.

Fate and Love

I Will Come to You

On this first full moon, late in the night I will come to you
When the moon beams hits the window you will see me call you
You will hear my whisper to come to the clearing
The pull of my desire will bring an urgency in you
My memory will be ever present in your mind
You will leave your bed and find me
For I have called you this night.

The moonlight will shine against my body
You will feel my desire as you come closer to me
For I have summoned you this night
My hair of fire cascades down my back
You can smell my desire in the air
All is still this night

You stand before me, my fingers touch your warm skin.
I take your hand and place it on my breast.
I slowly move my hands to your thighs
I can feel you tremble
You move your hand slowly between my thighs and you feel my desire.
Your power rises before me
You lie on the earth; I mount you and feel your power deep inside me.
The fire which is ours explodes
The rain falls and I feel the wetness of the rain on my face
The winds swirls around us and increases our pleasure
For we are one with ourselves and the elements

Our pleasure belongs to us.

We are the son and the daughter of the Goddess.
We have enjoyed her gift.
You have come to me as you have in the past
You will come to me again and again
For my desire will draw you to me
For I am a Witch and my desire is you.

I will wait

On this cool night I feel warmth

His touch on my body raises the heat within

The gentle caress of his hand brings us close

You came to me this night

We were drawn to this mountain top

Moon beams led the way

In our Sacred Space we have come

Heather sways in the wind

Feet bare, we feel the power of the earth

Slowly making their way the Fae come

They have been called this night

For what will be done

Our lives will be changed

My love for this warrior will remain

Time will not distance us

For we have known each other since dawn

We stand on the mountain

Moon beams dance on the loch

This beauty is forever

He has brought his power for us

He raises me to heights unknown

I see all that can be seen

The unknown is known

I am strong under his light

We know no other

The call has come

We have answered our Goddess

Flutter of wings surrounds me

Gently, I lie upon the earth

Wind swirls around me

My gown floats beneath me

My arms raised, I call for my lover

Sweet sound of the pipes can be heard in the distance

Oh, how I want him

His voice which is so engaging

His hands which are so caring

The arms which hold me so close

My heart breaks knowing he will soon leave

For the time has come to raise arms

Our land will remain free

No storm will dissolve our resolution

But, blood will be shed

Mothers will weep

Wives will clutch their breasts in sorrow

We will bury our men and sons

I will be still

I will wait on this spot

I am strong in your love

I am not ready for you to leave me

You raise me to unknown courage

I am more than I can be in your light

I will hold our land

Sword in hand we will be firm

So, say your goodbyes

I will wait ...

Children of the Goddess

You step from the shadows
I have seen you there before
You wait for a sign
I know why you have come here this night
I have called you this night

I sent my power to the wind to summon you this Full Moon
You stand before me and wait
I take my hand and run it over your body
I feel you quiver at my touch
I remove my linen shift, it drops to the ground
I stand naked before you

The Goddess has called her Witches
She has called us to join in the Great Ritual
We will dedicate ourselves to her this night, as we have done in the past
You have waited for me,

We are known to each other
Our lives have been intertwined in the past, now in the present
You take me this night
Your power reaches deep into me, it fills me with desire

We have joined as Witches do, no shame. Just pleasure
The night is filled with the desire of Witches
As children of the Goddess we know who we are

And the power we have this night

We rule ourselves and the night

We go into the night as Children of the Goddess

For we are Witches and the earth belongs to us....

Longing

Tears fall cold on my cheeks.

I press against the glass,

Looking for you.

Will you return?

I Know You

I can feel your breath, my back turned to you
I can feel your warmth flow to me
I can sense your touch
I can feel your power
All known to me

I hear you call for me
I hear your words of passion
I hear your words of love
I hear your words of desire and want

I know you, and want what you want
I know your heart, I see the truth
I know the passion that you bring
I know the power you have for me

For we are Witches, we have known each other in the past.
For we are Witches, we will know each other in the future
For we are Witches, we are the children of the Goddess
For we are Witches, we know our power

The Goddess

The rain falls as I stand in the clearing

I feel the wetness through my shift as it clings close to my body

The cool breeze makes me shiver under the full moon

I hear the music from the trees as they sway in the breeze

The spider's web glimmers under the moonlight

I feel the earth cool, wet beneath me

The Goddess has called me this night

She has called me for you

She has seen us in the past

She wants us to join in the present

We are her children and she guides us to each other

You come from the darkness of the trees

You walk to me as I stand before the Goddess

I know what you want from me

You lower my shift from my shoulders; it falls to the ground

I feel your breath on my neck

You turn me to face you, as the moonlight hits your body

I stand naked before you and you touch my body.

You touch what belongs to you and what we share.

You reach for me and pull me close

I feel your power and desire this night

I know what is expected of me.

I remove your shirt, tracing your body with my hands

You remove your pants, we stand naked before each other

We stand naked before the Goddess

You lie on the earth, waiting for me

I slide on to you, feeling all that you are this night

Feel your energy as it rises within me.

I feel your energy enter me

Your body rises to meet mine, our power combines

I feel you deep in my body; the gift from the Goddess has been released

You pull me closer to you. I feel the fire of your body

The Goddess has given us this gift.

She has given us this joining as a dedication to her light

We are her children

She has given herself to us this night

We have become one with her.

She is the light of our path

We walk this path together

She will protect us from all

She is the light in the darkness

We as Witches know her and stand before her as her children

We as Witches are the children of the light

We as Witches belong to her and ourselves

We as Witches will be with each other forever

We as Witches lower our heads to her light

We as Witches go forth with her love and protection

This Night

The moon has risen this night and it is full

There is a cool breeze

The rain is gentle as it falls

I stand naked before the Goddess on the mountain

I hear the pipes as they call to me

The earth is cold under my feet

You come to me, wrapping your cloak around me

I feel the warmth of your hands and body

I feel your desire as you touch me

My breasts rise at your touch

My thighs quiver with your touch

I feel the wetness inside of me

My body is ready as you remove your cloak

It falls to the earth

Gently, you lower me upon your open cloak

You open my thighs and slide into me

I feel your power and urgency

I respond to your energy

My body rises to reach yours

We have been given the greatest gift of all

We are Witches and on this night

We have dedicated ourselves to the Goddess

We have been joined for all time by her gift

This night has been ours

This night will always be ours

TIME

We have traveled time

You came from the past to find me

You claimed me in the present

You will look for me in the future

I came from the past to wait for you

You found me in the present

I will wait for you in the future

You whisper to me now

You send your words to me

You call me to you

I hear your whisper. I look for you

I feel your words. I turn to you

I know your call. I find you

I touch your face, a face I know

I brush your hair back, I know you

I touch your body and remember you

You touch the back of my neck and I know you

You touch my breasts. I know you

You touch my thighs. I know you

My body rises to your touch

My heart beats rapidly as you touch me

My thighs quiver with excitement at your touch

You take me this night

You take me on the cold earth

You take me as the moon rises.

Your power enters me and I feel the fire

Your power enters me and I feel the rain

Your power enters me as the wind brushes my body

We are the Son and Daughter of the Goddess

We are joined for all time

We are Witches and know our past

We are Witches and know the present

We are Witches and know our destiny

I have loved you in the past

I love you now

I will love you in the future

I knew you in the past

I know you in the present

I will wait for you in the future my love

For I am a Witch and the daughter of the Goddess

And all that I envision will be mine

Joining of Witches

I can hear his words asking for me
I can hear his thoughts call to me
I can hear the whispers of his desire for me

He has found me...

We stand before the Goddess
We stand under the clear sky
We stand in the grassy knoll
We stand in full awareness of nature

The animals gather around us

Our hawk is perched on a tree limb
Our stag stands near us and watches our movements
Our black cat stands next to me, her green eyes gaze deep into me
Our wolf stands full with her power and protection

They are gifts from the Goddess.
They are of nature, just as we

I am still, he calls the corners
I am still, he calls the elements
I am still, he draws down the moon
I am still, he call the Goddess for us
I am still, he places his hand in mine

He wants to be with me
He wants to hold me

He wants to feel me

He wants to know me

He wants to join with me

He takes me deep in the forest.

He takes me to a clearing surrounded by pines.

He takes me to the edge of this world under the moonlight

I touch his face and I feel his emotions

I touch his thighs and I feel his power

I touch his lips and we kiss, warm and sweet

I touch his back and pull him to me as I lie upon the ground.

He touches my neck, I feel his warmth

He touches my lips, he feels my desire

He touches my thighs, they quiver

He touches my breast, feels my passion

I have drawn him onto me as he draws the moon onto us

He slides into me, I feel his power

He slides into me, I feel his energy

He slides into me and feels my wetness

He slides into me, as I rise to his power

There is stillness around us for we are

Witches and have been joined.

Witches

As the sun sets
The moon rises.
We are called.
Gathering deep in the forest
Our capes flap in the wind.
Hoods covering our head
As we form our circle
Hand in hand we take our places.
The elements are called forth:
Wind, rain, earth and fire.
We are filled with their energy.
In a low chant
We call for our Mother.
The Goddess answers our call,
She stands before us,
Center in our circle.
We lower our heads to her grace.
Our circle is filled with her love.
Energy flows from her to us.
Slowly we rise;
Our feet no longer touch the ground.
Wind rips through the trees.
Flames raise high from the fire.
Rain beats on the earth below
Yet, we remain dry.
Power transfers from Sister to Sister.
The Goddess's influence is felt.
Sounds from the forest fill the air.
All is alive.
Energy fills all there,
We know who we are,
The Witches of the present.
Those long past have joined us.
We know our beginning.
We know our past.
We know our future,
Witches now and forever.

We Are Known

She has given us this joining as a dedication to her light

We are her children and we know all that she can be

She has given herself to us this night

We have become one with her this night

She is the light of our path

We walk this path together

She will protect us from all

She is the light in the darkness

We as Witches know her and stand before as her children

We as Witches are the children of the light

We as Witches belong to her and ourselves

We as Witches will be with each other forever

We as Witches lower our heads to her light

We as Witches go forth with her love and protection

Scottish Night

I stand in the ruins of the castle
I stand as the sun sets and the moon rises
I stand watching the waves on the loch through the window
I stand as the music of the lone piper reaches me
I stand viewing the greenness of the mountain
I stand as the heather sways in the breeze
I stand while the beauty of the land encircles me with warmth
I feel him walk to me
I hear him call me
I know this man who comes
I see him walk towards me
I know the kilt of the clan
I see the *sgain dubhs* as it reflects the light of the moon
I have given him my heart
He has my dreams
He is who I belong to
He is in my heart and will always be there
He is my past
He is my present
He is my future
Here is my heart which I give to you
These are my dreams which I give to you
Here is my being, I give it freely to you
The moon shines full and we become one ...

Gift

Naked, I stand before you
My linen shift lies at my feet
The earth is damp beneath me from a late mist
Flames raise high beneath the cauldron
I feel the wind blow through my hair
You take your cape to cover my shoulders
Standing near me I feel your force
From the distance I hear the pipes
A lone piper stands beneath the moon
His music fills the loch
I have answered your call
Your words have traveled for me to come
You have touched my heart
My soul is yours
I have known you from the past
I feel your touch in the night as I lie alone
In this space I will become yours
Time can not keep us apart
I remain yours
For your power will transform us
We will find all that is to be
The Goddess has led us to this night
My hands trace your body
I shiver with excitement
Your energy rises as you enter me
I have never known such pleasure
We will ride the wind
High and free
Our pleasure remains ours
Free to enjoy each other
Our desires entwine each others'
A gift from the Goddess
For we are her children
What we share belongs to her
We celebrate her glory
As we become one
She blessed this night for us

Seasonal and Lunar

Imbolc

We can feel the sun on us.
We have come to celebrate.
We have the power to see the future.
We have come this day to our Blessed Space.
We sense the earth's life beneath our feet.
We feel the wind on our skin.
We raise the flames from fire.
We feel rain fall gently to earth.

Brighid calls for her daughters and sons.

We call for the corners to open.
We call for our Sisters and Brothers from the past.
We call for our Siblings to present themselves.
We call for the lamb and ewes.
We call for the blackthorn to bloom
We call for the Sun to shine her life force.
We call forth our purification.
We call forth our power

Brighid makes herself known to us.

On this day we open the veil
On this day we see into the unknown.
On this day we turn the cards.
On this day we read the stones.
On this day we scry.
On this day we look deep into our palms
On this day we can see all.
On this day we know what is known.

Brighid has come for her daughters and sons.

We stand before the Goddess
We stand on the ground so green.
We stand beneath the Ash
We stand before the earth's blooms.

We stand with our Sisters and Brothers.
We stand with our arms raised to the Goddess.
We stand as her daughters and sons.
We stand as Sisters and Brothers to all.

Brighid lights our way

On this day we go forward with her love.
On this day we release our gifts to the wind.
On this day we draw on the earth's life.
On this day we call forth the rain.
On this day we seed our life force.
On this day we send our energy forth.
On this day we bring forth life.
On this day we claim our gifts

We close our space.
We go forward in pure love.

Life continues and so do we.

Ostara

Flowers flow from our altar
Bright colors of spring fill the room
Each of us has placed a bud in the cauldron
We wait for the rebirth
We wait for the renewal
We have freed ourselves from the icy prison
Winter is in the past
We form our circle
A chain of spring flowers bind us
We find the joy in the sun
The Goddess has shown that light conquers dark
We stand in her light and love
We have washed and removed all that is negative
Our capes of light blue reflect the light
Our Sisters and Brothers stand with us
We praise the Goddess for all she has done
We bow to her presence
She fills us with her glory
We are her daughters and sons
Our lives have been renewed in her light
Blessings to the Witches near and far

Bloodlines

Beltane brought us together.
But I had seen you years before.
Looking deep into the flames I saw your face.
I could feel your want.
Keeping myself for you, I waited.
With the strength of a warrior you came to me.
You found me and we became one.
Your strong arms would keep me safe.
Your love kept us warm.
Long winter nights were filled with our passion.
In the dark I would reach and find you.
With your protection we lived in peace.
Our passion brought forth our children.

On the Winter Solstice, Rhiannon was born.
My grandmother had named her with a whisper.
The first born of our brood, she had the gift of sight.
Flames and water would bring the visions.
The Fae watched her birth.
They would protect her eternally.
She would claim the realm of the Fae as hers.
They would carry out her desires.
Her devotion to them would only parallel her love
      for the Goddess.
With her power she would stand strong with her sisters.
Her village claimed her as theirs.
She brought them joy and laughter.
I would watch as she performed the rituals of passage
      to become one with the Circle.
The call of the Fae would bring her to the forest.
Deep within, she would dance around the fire.
Their wings fluttering with joy at her grace
With elegance she would fly with the Fae.
Their bond would remain.
I would see my sister in her eyes.

On the Full Moon of Beltane, I bore Brighid

Moon energy filled the room.
Our breath was taken away by the moon's influence.
Rays danced against the walls as she came forth.
She was our child of moons fervor and force.
She took the name of my Goddess.
The brightness of her red hair shone as her grandmother
        presented her to the Moon.
The Moon drew down to her tiny body.
She carried my gifts in her hand
Brighid would have power over the Elements.
Wind would come when called.
Rain fell as she wished.
Earth would rise beneath her steps.

She controlled fire with a raise of her hands.
Imprinted on her consciousness was the wisdom of
        those who came first.
Knowledge was her power.

Moon's darkness brought us Kirsten.
During the dark of the moon I brought forth
        my raven haired daughter.
Eyes of blue, she mirrored her father.
She would claim her father's clan.
Most of her was him.
She was a true daughter of a warrior.
As a maiden sword bearer, she would fight next to her father.
Fighting seen and unseen dangers.
In time she would lead our clan
Her courage and daring would become legend.
Her sword forged by her father would carry her into battle.
One forged of the blood of our people.
Trained since childhood she would control its power
Kirsten would hold all its authority
A shield made of bronze was forged by my people
Twenty seven circles inlaid in the shield for each year
        since her birth.
The sign of the Goddess laid center of the shield.
Blessed by all the women, power rose as she held the shield.
Men would follow our daughter.

She would lead them to glory.
My heart fell each tine she mounted her steed.

She went with my Blessings.
She went with my prayers.
My heart was born on Imbolc.
Jamie came into our life as the Moon waxed
I could hear the wolf's howl on the wind.
I heard the sound of hooves as the stag came to me.
Hoots from the owls filled the air.
Our horses neighed and pranced.
Growls were heard in the distance.
The flutter of wings
Thumping of the mountain hares
Chirps from red squirrels filled the room.
His sisters were eager to hold him their arms.
He would be the center of their lives.
By the grace of the Goddess he would command the animals
For his connection was deep with them.
Their words became his
With great dignity they bowed before him.
He would be cunning as fox,
Wise as the owl,
Swift as the stag,
Strong as the bear,
Clever as the wolf.
His domain covered the forest.
Pinewoods of the Caledonian were his home.
His soul lay deep in the woods.

Our children would carry our bloodline.
They would explore their powers.
Each one growing into their own.
Our lives would continue through them.
The Goddess would watch them,
She gave them her light and grace.
She blessed their lives and ours.
We would remain.
Our village claimed them as theirs.

Litha

Life giving power surrounds us
The Goddess will soon give life
Our earth is filled with the promise of growth
It is a time of joy and celebration
Yet, there is a whisper that dark will soon come
Light has reached its power
The Sun power begins to wane
Our Oak King is rich in abundance
But soon his brother will reign
The decent begins with the Holly King
Bonfires are alight
We find each other and prepare for the night
None will sleep
We wait for the sunrise
We dance with abundance
Leaping high through flames
The smells of healing herbs fill the air
We prepare for what will come
Our homes prepared for the darkness
As we make our bread we pray that the Goddess
       fills our homes
Wheat from our fields changed to grain
Mixed by loving hands
Placed in the fire to cook
Ale, honey cakes, and bread fill the pantry,
Sprigs of rosemary hung from the rafters
The wheel of life continues

Mabon

Our Goddess has changed from mother to crone.
She holds all our knowledge and wisdom
Her insight radiates from her to us
Her consort, our God is present
He prepares for death then re-birth
This cycle will continue
As the fields empty
Our homes are filled with the harvest.
As we wait for the second harvest.
We watch the beauty of the land change
Red, orange, maroon, brown and gold fill the forest
Day and night are equal
A balance between the two
Light and dark maintained
We feel the cold as it creeps into our homes.
Our altars are prepared, covered with pine cones, acorns.
We wear stones of sapphire
Their brilliance dances around the room
Vines of ivy flow
Horns of plenty overflow
We give thanks for our bounty
We share our Blessings with the Goddess
We share our Blessings with the God
We share our bounty with our family
We have cleansed our home
We have prepared ourselves
The hearth is cleaned and prepped
Logs of alder and ash are afire.
The cauldron boils with potatoes, carrots and onions
Aroma from honeysuckle, myrrh, rose and sage fill our homes
A call to gather has been heard
We gather to celebrate
Sisters stand hand in hand
Candles light our space
We bow before she who is present
We accept her love and protection
Whispers of prayers can be heard

Each of us ask for her Blessings
We know that she will bless us
For we follow her path
We follow her grace
The yearly cycle is ending
We look forward to the renewal of life
We share wine and the bounty of the earth
We close our night with prayer
We close our night in peace
We close our night in harmony with all
As Witches we belong to All That Is
We belong to all that will be
Blessed Be

Wisdom

Through the ages I have traveled
I have seen all there is to know
I have entered the space that lies untouched
My power has bridged time
Energy has filled the void
Their voices can be heard
I know what they have been taught
Their memories travel with me
For I know who they are
Our circle remains unbroken
For they call to me
I have come freely to know them
They have passed their knowledge to me
I can feel their thoughts
Their wisdom is mine
From time to time
From Witch to Witch
We are one ...

Season of Change

I feel the change on my body
The wind blows. I feel the power
Leaves change. The Goddess has painted the earth in color
Sunlight peeks behind the clouds. The rays hit my window

Our animal friends prepare for winter
They gather for the cold months
Food is stored, their coats thicken
Some have left to find warmer ground

We feel the call of change
The New Year is upon us
We call on our ancestors
We call on each other

We gather for the rite
We gather as Sisters
We gather under the full moon
We gather with our hands in each other's

I step forward and call on the Goddess
I stand in the center and am encircled by the power of the Witches
I turn and see those I care about
I hear them whisper their prayers

We raise our voice high to the Mother Goddess

We send our wishes and prayers
May she Bless each of us
May she send her love to us

We call on each of us to come
We call on the Blessings of the earth
We call on each other for the power of the Sisterhood

May the Season bring you all your hopes and dreams
May the Season bring you fortune and health

May the Season bring you love and comfort
May the Season bring you joy and laughter

To My Sisters ... my love to all
May your home be filled with warmth and joy

In the darkness there is light
In the silence there is sound
In the pain there is comfort
In the fear there is safety

In the distance there is oneness
In the tear there is joy
In the loss we are found
In the hate we find love

In the Sisterhood we have the Goddess
For all comes from her and all goes to her
She will give and she will take
We learn all from her

Stand strong and all will be well

As it is above so be below

Yule

The longest night has come.
In the darkness we celebrate light.
The Goddess has given life.
We are reborn in her light.
The sun will rise
His light will cover us.
For we are his children
Together with the Goddess all is right.
Our lives continue under their grace.
We will know life again
For we are also reborn
Under the snow there is life
For as the Sun raises so do we
Our life is short on earth
But as their children our life continues
We know life ... for we remain

Moon Rise, Sunset

As the Moon rises the Sun sets
We send out our power of Sisterhood for them
      To claim all that they are

As the Moon rises the Sun sets
We send the power of the Sisterhood to all
      To be all that they are

As the Moon rises the Sun sets
We send the power of the Sisterhood that our
      Sisters find prosperity

As the Moon rises the Sun sets
We send our power to the Sisterhood that they
      will find joy and love.
As the Moon rises and the Sun sets
We send our power of the Sisterhood

I turn East and ask for guidance.
I turn South and ask for success.
I turn West and ask for happiness.
I turn North and ask for love.

As we stand before the Goddess we humble ourselves
      to her majesty.
As we stand before the Goddess we humble ourselves
      before our Sisters.
As we stand before the Goddess we humble ourselves
      before the power of the Moon.
As we stand before the Goddess we humble ourselves
      to the beauty of life.

I stand under the Full Moon and feel her rays fall on me
I stand under the Full Moon and feel the gentle breeze
I stand under the Full Moon and feel the earth beneath me
I stand under the Full Moon and feel the spring shower

I look towards the Alder and feel the magick of the fairies
I look towards the Alder and feel my spirit grow
I look towards the Alder and hear the Old Ones
I look towards the Alder and see my future

As I come tonight before the Goddess and my Sisters
    I ask for patience in my life.
As I come tonight before the Goddess and my Sisters
    I ask for healing.
As I come tonight before the Goddess and my Sisters
    I ask for comfort.
As I come tonight before the Goddess and my Sisters
    I ask for joy.

I raise my arms pulling the Moon power to me
I raise my arms calling on my Sisters
I raise my arms to call on Wise Ones
I raise my arms to call on nature

For I am a daughter of the Goddess
For I am a Sister to all

For I am the protector
For I am all and all is mine.

Full Moon

The Moon has risen and the glow comes into our circle.
My Sisters join hands and bow their heads
As the Goddess is called to us.

I call on the Wind to present her self
I call on the Fire to rise high from our cauldrons.
I call on the Rain to fall gently upon us.
I call on the Earth, who is mother to us all.

I turn to the East and summon the Witches
I turn to the South and summon my Words
I turn to the West and summon the Energy
I turn to the North and summon the Light

I make my circle of protection and bow as
I request the love and light of the Goddess.
I make my circle of protection and invite
      my Sisters to join the light.
I make my circle of protection
      and place my family there with me.
I make my circle of protection
      and place my animals with us.

I raise my arms to the Moon
      drawing down her energy.
I raise my arms to the Moon
      drawing down her light.
I raise my arms to the Moon
      drawing down her love.
I raise my arms to the Moon
      and drawn down her protection.

She is our Mother and I ask for her prayers

I pray for the families of my Sisters
I pray for the fulfillment of my destiny
I pray for the joy of life to fill my life

I pray for the protection of my Siblings and myself

Blessings to the birds in our skies
Blessings to animals that roam our lands
Blessings to creatures of the seas
Blessings to our pets, which love is constant

Joy to us and all of ours
Laughter that fills our lives
May we see the beauty around us
Find a passion that will live forever

I give my love and energy to my Sisters
I open my circle and release the joy
And peace from this gathering
I open my circle and release the Love
And Energy from this gathering
I open my circle and release
Our devotion to the Goddess

I thank the Goddess for her presence
I thank the Witches for their presence
I thank the Elements for their presence
I thank my Sisters for their presence

To All with my Love and Blessings

All is done...

Full Moon Ritual

The Full Moon ritual starts with forming the Circle. Each Sister takes the hand of her Sister next to her. The Circle is formed with our power. We ask our Sisters from the past to join us. As we bow before the Moon, we ask the Goddess to join us as we stand before our past, present and future.

Our words are sent on the Wind
Our words rise high as the Fire in our cauldron reaches the sky.
Our words blend into Mother Earth.
Our words flow, as the tides travel across the Water.

Your daughters stand before you
Our Sisters stand strong in the Light of the Moon
Your daughters stand in the power of the Moon
Our Sisters stand with each other as the Moon shines upon us

We pass a candle to each other.
We see the Love of each of our Sisters
We feel the power of the Moon as we drawn her to us
We watch as the power grows from the Earth and is drawn to us

Our Circle is strong with the Witches from the past
Our Circle grows as those from the past
        present themselves before us
Our Circle is joined by our animals
Our Circle draws down the Moon

Bless our families
Bless our Sisters
Bless our homes
Bless our lives

Bring prosperity to all
Bring health to those in pain
Bring the security of our jobs
Bring love to all

We send our love to those who have passed

We send our joy to those who have been released from pain
We send our power to those in need
We send our protection for those in fear

We open the cages and let them free
We open the cages to our minds
We open the cages of our hearts to find love and joy
We open the cages that keep us prisoners

Send the power of self confidence to our children
Send children to those who are childless
Send joy to those who can not find joy
Send security and safety to all

Keep our homes safe
Keep our lives filled with humor
Keep our families healthy and strong
Keep our Sisters safe

We ask that our prayers be filled
We ask that our lives be full
We ask that our Sisters find love and compassion
We ask for those who are held, to be set free

As we stand under the Full Moon
We thank the Goddess
As we stand under the Full Moon
We thank and release the Witches from the past
As we stand under the Full Moon
We thank and release the Elements
As we stand under the Full Moon
We thank and send forth our words

As we turn to each other we end this night with truth and love we release their hand. As we turn to each other we send prefect love and trust with this kiss. Our prayers have been sent to the wind. The Goddess has shown her love and light.
We release each other.
Blessed Be

Moon Rise

As the moon so bright and full rises in the sky
    we look upwards to see our Mother
As the wild ground phlox bloom to its glorious pink
    we look to see our Mother.
As the birds return and their voices fill the wind
    we look to see our Mother.

The burrows are empty and the animals roam the woods;
    our Mother is there.
The caves are empty as the bears roam the forest;
    our Mother is there.
The wolf has emerged and she takes her place on the ridge
    howling towards the wind;
    our Mother is there.

We feel drawn to the earth, our Mother calls us.
We feel drawn to the moon, our Mother calls us.
We feel the wind around us, our Mother calls us.

I stand before the moon and face my Mother.
I stand with arms reached out and face my Mother.
I stand humbled before her beauty and face my Mother.

I send the hopes of my family.

I send the prayers of my Sisters.
I send peace and love.

May she answer my prayers.
May she answer my hopes.
May she answer my wishes.

Blessings to my Sisters.
Blessings to our families.
Blessings to our animals.

All is done.
All is well.

Day's End

As the day ends the moon rises on the longest day of the year
    I stand before All That Is.
As the day ends I present myself before the Goddess.
As the day ends I present myself before the Sun God.
As the day ends I present myself before the Lady and the Lord.

    I reaffirm my dedication to all.
    I am bound to the old ways.
    I am one with all.

I stand under the Waxing Gibbous Moon to receive its light.
I stand under the Waxing Gibbous Moon to give thanks.
I stand under the Waxing Gibbous Moon to call on nature.
I stand under the Waxing Gibbous Moon to see who I am.

The honeysuckle surrounds me as I stand before all.
The Oak trees in all their majesty surround me in my space.
The animals have come and stand with me.
The smell of myrrh fills the wind as it burns in my cauldron.

I call on the Witches of the North to present themselves.
I call on the Witches of the East to present themselves.
I call on the Witches of the South to present themselves.
I call on the Witches of the West to present themselves.

    The elements of Fire, Water, Earth and Air are called
    for their power, light and protection.

The Lady and her Lord present themselves
    as I stand humbled before them.

"What is your request my daughter?"

I request for myself, my family and my Sisters
    Love,
    Health,
    Joy,

Humor,
Security,
Prosperity.

I request that those in pain find comfort.
I request that those who cry in the night find comfort.
I request for those who live in fear to find safety.
I request that our animals are free from harm.
I request that those who are cold find warmth.

I bow before the Lady and her Lord, for I am known to them.

My work has been sent and I rest...

Watchtowers

I call on the Watchtowers of the North
I call on the Watchtowers of the East
I call on the Watchtowers of the South
I call on the Watchtowers of the West

I call on the Witches of the past
I call on the Witches of this time
I call on the Witches to come
I call on those who have gone before me

I ask for the Goddess to show her light
I ask for the Goddess to show her love
I ask for the Goddess to show her protection
I ask for the Goddess to stand with me

I stand under the Full Moon
      and send my energy to the four corners

I call on the elements of Fire, Water, Earth and Fire
      To do my bidding

I command the fire to rise from my cauldron.
I command the tides to rise as I stand under the moon.
I command the earth to feel my soul upon it.
I command the air to send my words to my Sisters.

I pray that we hear what can not be heard.
I pray we hear the voices of those who can not speak.
I pray we feel the pain of those who suffer in silence.
I pray we feel compassion for those in need.
I pray we stand for those who are unable.

We who have the power
Need to be the power for those who do not.

May the children find sleep in comfort.
May the elderly find compassion and comfort.

May the animals be free from cages and pain.
May those in pain find relief.
May those who live in fear find safety.
May those who cry in the night be loved.

As I and my sisters stand before the power of the Full Moon
      And the Goddess.
We who serve are comforted by the love that she gives us daily.

I close my circle as I thank the Witches
      of the North, East, South and West.

I bow my head before the Mother Goddess
And thank her for her presence
I take the hands of my Sisters and
Release our energy to the wind
I bow my head before the Mother Goddess and
Thank her for all she has given.
I take the hands of my Sisters and
Release their light to the moon.

As we have received, so we release.

As it is above, so be below.

Blessed Be.

Moon Power

By the power of the Moon I stand before thee
With my sisters I bow before your light
And ask for your Blessings
We ask with the power of three times three
That you grant our prayer
We ask with the power of the Sisterhood to be heard

We call on the energy force of nature
To send our power to each of us
We call on the love of the Goddess to take us in her arms
We call on our Sisters past to stand as our witnesses
We call on those we love who have passed to share this night

May love and joy fill our lives
May prosperity come to all our lives
May our wishes be fulfilled

I turn to the East and call on my Sisters
I turn to the South and call on nature
I turn to the West and call on the Witches from the past
I turn to the North and call on the light of the Goddess

As the Moon rays fall on me, I feel her energy.
As the Moon rays fall on my Sisters I feel their energy.
As the Moon rays fall on me I feel the light of the Goddess.
As the Moon rays fall on me I feel the power of the earth.
As the Moon rays fall on me
I know I am a daughter of the Goddess.

I know what it means to be a daughter.

I bow to the light, the energy and beauty of the Goddess.
I feel her embrace.
I feel my hand in my Sisters'.
I know the power we have.
I know the responsibility.

I bless those in my life

I bless those who are gone from me
I hold dear my animals
I know those gone are close to me
I bless my Sisters

I thank the Goddess for hearing my prayers
I thank the force of energy for its power
I thank my Sisters
I thank my family and friends

For all is done ...

Moon Dance

Dance under the moon.

Rise to her gifts.

Watch the flames increase.

Feel the earth beneath.

Know the wind is yours.

Catch the rain.

Dance under the moon.

Circle Power

I stand before the Goddess as her daughter
My head bowed before her love and light
I do not stand alone
My Sisters stand with me
My family stands with me
The Witches from the past are present
I humbly ask for her presence in my home
I raise my hands and extend love to all
I ask the Goddess to send her protection to me
I ask her to encircle my home
I ask her to hold me close

With the power of my Circle, I cast out evil.
    Return it to its source.
With the power of the Goddess, I cast out pain.
    Return it to its source.
With the power of the Witches, I cast out hate.
    Return it to its source.

I turn East
I turn South
I turn West
I turn North

Under the Fullness of the Moon my home is safe
Under the Fullness of the Moon I am safe
Under the Fullness of the Moon my family is safe
Under the Fullness of the Moon my Sisters are safe

The Goddess holds me and I am safe...

Blessed Be

My Daughter

I stand before the Goddess naked and I am known
I stand before the Goddess, my head lowered to her grace
I stand before the Goddess, she knows my heart
I stand before the Goddess, seeking her guidance

I feel the pain that that encroaches on me.
       I am filled with despair.
I feel the pain that surrounds my heart
I feel the pain that has taken possession of my soul
I feel the pain and see no escape

As despair takes over, I hear a whisper
As despair takes over, I feel the wind
As despair takes over, I feel the rain
As despair takes over, I feel the earth beneath me
As despair takes over, I feel the fire of the cauldron

I feel arms that wrap around me and keep me warm
I feel the love that encircles me
I feel that calm that comes from the earth
I hear words of comfort
I hear a soft voice of love

This is the Goddess, for I am her daughter.
This is the Goddess who takes my pain from me.
This is the Goddess who reminds me of who I am
This is the Goddess who I belong to
This is the goddess and I am her creation
This is the Goddess who I am dedicated to

For I am Witch and her daughter

Natural Forces, Prayers & Devotions

Natural Forces

My Sisters

I enjoy the harmony of natural forces without effect or strain. I am part of and belong to what surrounds me. I take joy each day that comes. I experience the presence of healing that brings me strength. I am the cord that maintains the past and present. I send my will to the wind and it travels to my Sisters. They send back to me their love and power. With all that I am, I am wise. The force of nature is respected and praised. I call on fire, water, earth, and air to do my bidding. They answer and we become one. I have become a force of nature.

A Witch's Prayer

As the season changes we feel the change

We bless all that surrounds us and wait for the veil to open

The time has come;
We call on those who have passed to present themselves

Our past stands before us

We pray for their spirits to be free.
We pray for their journey to be peaceful.
We pray they send their blessings.
We pray they find comfort.

The Evening

The evening has descended and all is still
I hear my heart beat as I wait for the moon's fullness
I can hear the wind as it travels to me
I stand in the clearing waiting for what is to come
I stand naked before the Goddess as she knows who I am

I feel my Sisters as they come for me
I feel their love as they encircle me
I hear the thoughts of those who have gone before me
I hear their Blessings as they are sent to me

I know what is asked of me
I know what is expected of me
I have become one with the past, present and future

I am a daughter of the Goddess
I am a Sister to those who stand with me
I am a Witch, past, present and future

We Know

We know in our hearts the truth
We know in our hearts pure joy
We know in our hearts love
We know in our hearts laughter
We know in our hearts what compassion is
We know in our hearts kindness

We stand before the Goddess open to her will and love
We feel all that comes to us

I Am

I am more than what anyone expects
I am more than what the world sees
I am more than what I show you
I am more than what can be
I am more than a woman
I am part of the earth and the earth is part of me
I feel the best when I am working the earth
I feel fulfilled when I see the growth of the earth
I smell the beauty of the earth when it rains
My self and my Sisters, we are of the earth
The earth is our Mother
I am more than what is seen and more to come

Witch

In the dark of the night as I try to sleep,
I hear the words, "Witch, Witch, you're a Witch."

In the dark of the night as I try to sleep,
I hear the cries of pain from my Sisters long past.

In the dark of the night as I try to sleep,
I hear the pleas from the innocent for mercy as they are tortured.

In the dark of the night as I try to sleep,
I feel their fear as they are locked in the dark and damp cells.

In the dark of the night as I try to sleep,
I feel the pain that my Sisters experienced
At the hands of the judges.

In the dark of the night as I try to sleep,
I feel the cold chains on my hands.

In the dark of the night as I try to sleep,
I see the flames as they engulf my Sisters.

In the dark of the night as I try to sleep,
I feel alone.

In the dark of the night as I try to sleep
My Sisters stand vigil by my bed.

In the dark of the night as I try to sleep...
Light comes to shine in my room.
I feel the embrace of the Goddess and I know I am safe.

The Growth of Pain

I feel the pain deep in my soul.
I feel it in my heart.
I feel it each day that comes.
I feel it each day as it ends.

You said we were to be with each other always.
You said we had been together in the past.
You said we would be with each other in present.
You said you would find me in the future.
You said we would always be together.

He told me the Goddess had brought us to each other.
He told me the Goddess had sent him to me.
He told me the Goddess had made us for each other.

You claimed my heart.
You claimed my soul.
You claimed my memories.
You claimed my body.

I gave you my heart.
I gave you my soul.
I gave you my memories.
I gave you my body.

You vowed to protect now.
You vowed to protect me always.
You vowed to protect even when you were gone.

You vowed to protect with your life.

I gave you all that I had.

I gave you the true me.

I gave you what no one ever saw.

I gave you my trust.

You took it all and left.

You took my trust.

You took my love.

You took my heart.

What I found were my Sisters.

What I found was my power.

What I found was the love of the Goddess.

What I found was myself.

What I found was my strength.

What I found was what you could not take or destroy.

What I found was the Goddess within me.

What I found was me...

Blessings

The sun is setting
I prepare for my blessing
I have gathered my candles and they soon will be lit
My altar is dressed and flowers placed
My words swirl in my mind and heart
There is a breeze to carry my prayers to those in need
The energy comes from my Sisters and the Goddess
It is a good night to do work

So it starts...

I stand in the rays of the moon
I call on the Goddess
I ask for her presence
I ask for her Blessing

She stands before me
I am humbled by her light
My heart swells with her love
I know I am safe

She knows me
She knows my prayers
She knows my heart
She will guide my life

For I am the daughter of the Goddess

Dedication to the Goddess

The Goddess brings us no more or less than we are to her
She is the power for us to find ourselves
She is the light that guides our ways
She is the hand that extends when we are lost
She finds our heart and soul
For she knows what we hide
She bears all for us
For she is Mother and we are child

Protection

As the dark descends, the light remains
For the Goddess will protect her daughter.
Do not fear the dark, for she is there.
Your protection comes from the Goddess.
Your Sisters stand with you.
Be not fearful.
Evil will not prevail.
Stand strong and let her words flow through you...

Known

Out of the dark
Out of the shadows
Out of the closet

Stand and be known...

Draw down the moon
Cast the energy
Work the magick

Stand and be known ...

Fear be gone
Hatred is shed
Dread is released

Stand and be known ...

Know who you are
Accept who you are
Walk your path

Stand and be known ...

For you are daughter
For you are a Sister
For you are a Witch

Stand and be known ...

Witching Hour

The time has come

Witching hour has begun as I am drawn
To a clearing in the forest

I stand still before the Goddess, our Mother

I can feel the stag's stare
As he watches me from a distance

I can feel the wind on my skin as it encircles me
And flows though my hair

I stand on the wet earth and feel the call

I stand before the Moon as she calls me

For I am Witch and her daughter

You Are Loved

Feel me in your heart
Feel me in your soul
Hear my thoughts
Hear my words
As a daughter of the Goddess
Know that I will always be with you
Know there is no distance between us
Know that you are loved...

Revealed

I stand before my Goddess and she sees my sadness and tears.
I stand before my Goddess and she sees my heart.
I stand before my Goddess and she sees my pain.
I stand before my Goddess and feel her arms around me.

I feel her comfort.
I feel her love.
I feel joy.

I know I am loved.

A Gift for You

May your day be filled with joy
May your day be filled with love
May your day be filled with comfort
May your day be filled with humor

May the Goddess show you her light with joy
May the Goddess show you her light with love
May the Goddess show you her light with comfort
May the Goddess show you her light with humor

A smile is sent to you
A hug is sent to you
A touch of love is sent to you

May the Moon shine on you this day and many more
May the Moon's power fill your home
May the Moon's light fill you soul

Your power grows as the Moon rises
Your power grows as your Sisters stand with you
Your power grows as the Goddess sends her words to you

A whisper comes to you ...
You are my daughter and I am here with you

Blessings on this day and many more

New Year Blessings

May your year be filled with joy.
May all your wishes come true.
May your heart be filled with the warmth of family.
May you find laughter.

May you see the smile in a baby's eyes.

May you know happiness.
May you find fulfillment.
May your dreams come true.
May you know the power of your self.
May you not know pain.
May you not know sadness.
May you see the beauty that surrounds you.
May your home be filled with friends.
May you find comfort.
May you not know darkness,
   and most of all,
May your heart be filled with love.

Pipes

I can hear the pipes on the wind
I see heather sway in the wind
I can hear the call for the Witches
As I stand near the forest's end I see them gather
They form a circle under the full moon
They raise their hands to the Lady and the Lord
I hear their prayers as they flow to me on the wind
I am called by their power
I am called by their prayers
I am one with all
For I am their Sister

My Sisters

As we make ready for the Full Moon
You can feel the Goddess within you
As you light your candle, you can feel her drawn to you
The magick surrounds you and your work begins.
For those whose voices have been silenced, be theirs.
Find comfort that your prayers are sent on the wind
Find hope that you have changed a life
Turn to the moon, raise your voice in love to the Goddess
Pray for those whose voices can not be heard.

For the birds in our skies
For the fish in the sea
For the animals that roam our forest, plains and deserts
For the animals that live in fear and pain
For our pets whose devotion is never ending
For the children who cry themselves to sleep
For the elderly who live in distress
For those who hunger is not a stranger
For those who live in fear
For those whose days are filled with darkness
For those who do not love or peace

We are her children and the voice of those who are unheard
Raise your voice loud and strong

For your power is one with all

Light

In the darkness there is light
In the silence there is sound
In the pain there is comfort
In fear there is safety
In the distance there is closeness
In the tear there is joy
In the loss we are found
In hate we find love
In the sisterhood we have the Goddess
For all comes from her and all goes to her
Stand strong and all will be well
As it is above so be it below

Sleep

I call on the Goddess and all her love
I call on the Goddess and her light
I call on her power
I call on the healing power of my Sisters
I send my power to my Sisters
I receive their love
I receive their power
I am now safe in my sleep

I walk through darkness

I walk through darkness and see her light
      She holds me tight
       I feel your love my mother

I walk through darkness and see her light
      She holds me tight
       I feel your love my mother

I walk through darkness and see her light
      She holds me tight
       I feel your love my mother

....Say three times nightly...

Spirits

Fae

The earth is cool as I sit beneath the birch.
Leaning against the truck I hear wings flutter.
Moon beams fall on the ground.
I have come this night to be close to the forest.
Calling on the Fae to come
They will join me this night.
We have known each other for years.
They came to me as a young girl.
I found them playing in the undergrowth.
I could feel them before they presented themselves.
Our people have known them for generations.
They have served us with their loyalty.
Causing misfortune on our enemies
Their skills unmatched to others
Invaders have caused them to hide in barrows and cairns.
Making their homes in the forest
They found safety in the underground.
Cautiously they come forward to us.
We shared our magick.
We shared our protection.
Each one fearing the invaders,
They wanted our home.
Forcing their ways on us.
Together we would survive.
Our survival depends on each other.
Quietly they made their way to our enemies' camps.
They would invade their sleep.
Paths of Fae caused death to those
    who traveled their way.
We sought out each other for continued existence.
We would not submit to the new ways.
Fighting for our homes
We keep our ways.
Now we have tranquility.
Our home fires burn with serenity.
I have come to be with my friends.
Gently I call for Morgan.

I hear the flutter of her wings and she comes forth.
The light from the moon shines on her wings.
They look like silver in the light.
Light blue out lines her body.
A pale green dress covers her feet.
It rustles as she comes to me.

Her hair falls around her shoulders.
She has not changed in all these years.
Standing before me she lowers her head.
I lower mine in return.
We have known each other for years.
She had fought next to me many a time.
Her family has walked with mine.
We have both aged, but our magick remains.
We speak to each other.
Our words are known to us only.
She has grown weary over the years.
We share this together.
From a distance we hear a song.
Her sisters sing for us.
They sing of our battles.
Their words tell of times past.
Times of triumph
We remember days past.
Our hearts are filled with joy.
Tears fall to the grown.
The forest bed glimmers as her sisters come forth.
I see the beauty of the Fae.
Their magick fills the forest.
Animals make their way towards us.
The air is filled with power.
Tree branches sway in the wind.
A light rain falls on us.
I feel the earth deep below me.
The Mother Goddess stands before us.
We bow to her glory.
Fae, Witch, and all know her splendor.
We are breathless before her.

She was called by All That Is.
She brings her Blessings to all.
We feel her brilliance fill us.
All her children stand before her.
The stag comes and lowers his head.
A lone wolf comes and bows before her.
Smaller animals come forward.
Each showing their respect
Our forest is filled with worship for the Goddess.
We will follow her way for eternity.
Death will not separate us.
We remain her children.
The light dances on us.
We find warmth in her light.
We find life in her splendor.
Going forth we take her love with us.
For we all are her children, Witch and Fae.
We remain as she leaves.
Together we remain for all times.

The Web

You formed a web to capture me
It glimmered in the moonlight
Rain drops glitter like silver under the moon

You called me to the web
You filled it with visions of love
You made it strong to hold me with your words

I came willingly due to your words
I came willingly to the sweet sound of your voice
As the spider with the butterfly

You captured me in your web of lies and deceit
You thought that I had become your captive
You thought that you could play with me
As the spider with the butterfly

You forgot that I am not alone
You forgot that I am a daughter of the Goddess
You forgot that I am a Witch

My Sisters came for me with silver scissors to cut me free
My Sisters came with fire from their cauldron
To burn this web of lies
My Sisters came with their love and light
To destroy all that is you

They came with their Light and Power
They came and destroyed your web of darkness
They came and I was free

We are Witches and protect our own

Stillness

There is a stillness that has covered the forest.
It weighs heavy in the air.
The sense of danger has filled the forest,
For a hunter has approached.
The call is raised,
Animals hide in fear.
The underbrush is used for cover.
The hunter's footsteps can be heard.
In the distance the wolf comes forth,
Slowly making his way towards the enemy.
He crouches low to the ground.
A low growl is heard.
He spies his foe.
Ready to pounce, he stands strong.
From the earth a being rises between them,
Her cape flapping in the wind.
She removes her right hand from under her cape.
Reaching towards the sky she brings down lightning.
Thunder breaks the stillness,
With her power she aims for the hunter.
He is frozen in fear.
She draws back her arm,
With a flick of her elbow he is gone.
A smell of sulfur fills the air.
Sun rays fall to ground.
Sounds of nature fill the forest,
Life has resumed.
The Witch has shown her authority over all.

Grace of Spirit

Let your arms open wide.

Feel them inside.

Spirits come to you.

Hear their words.

They whisper in the night.

As a choir we hear them,

Singing their desires,

Telling their stories,

The sweet sounds of innocence.

On the wind they lift us.

Knowing who they are,

We are filled with their grace.

Releasing

Lonely, I stand on the mountain top
Here under the full moon I have come
I seek my love
My resolve remains undaunted
The sweet sound of the pipes flow on the wind
The music surrounds me
I look towards the sky and count the stars
Night lights beam off the loch
This night is filled with prayers
Lovers stand before their fires
Silently their desires come forth
They released them to find their way
Each one knowing
They face the fires and look deep into the flames
Flames leap from the hearth
We have released our power
Sent on the wind to those in need
Love remains eternal
It fills my heart with a joy and a sadness
The battle rages
Our freedom in balance
Warriors have been sent
They left with a command not seen before
We stand close as they march forth
Each one of us will work our magick
Swords and spear blessed by the Goddess
Their lives have been placed before the Goddess
We will wait ...

Claiming Victory

Slowly, I rest my body against Father Oak
I listen for their voices
Now I will call for my power to rise
For I am one with them
Why do they hide from me?
Those who chose to fight
Reaching into Mother Earth I gather her authority

Slowly, the dusk descends upon me
I hear voices from the underbrush
Now will they come before me?
Soul for Soul
For I am the answer to the call
Those who have chosen to stand with me
Reaching for the Moon, I claim her as mine

Slowly, I unsheathe my sword
I hear foot steps closing in around me
Now they must show themselves to me
Soul for Soul
For I am the one to stand and lead
Come ... those who will stand with me
Reaching into the Wind I claim her energy

Slowly, they have made their way to me
I hear their heart beat in unison
Now we will go forward
Soul for Soul
For I have been chosen
Their strength becomes one with mine
Reaching into the loch I claim her power

Slowly, we march forward
I hear the enemy
We have come in force
Soul for Soul
For the day belongs to us
Freedom lies within our grasp
Reaching out my sword I claim the day

Soul Piper

In this hour of the night
I have been called
To become one
The sun has sent
A season of change
The shade has taken over
See the river flow
Standing on her bank
I call for her
On the wind a piper plays
Music flows from the loch
It feeds my soul
Soon we will gather

Light

Light Wills Out

I feel the cold come through the walls.
The darkness surrounds me.
I am covered with despair.
My fears have surfaced.

My tattered shawl covers my bare shoulders.
I hear their foot steps.
I push my self to the corner of the cell.
Praying they have not come for me.

Rats fight for bits of food near me.
Spiders enter from the openings in the walls.
They climb the steep walls.
I sense they seek light and freedom.

Foot steps come closer to my cell.
I cringe against the wall.
My bare sheet covered by straw.
Fear and cold have overcome me.

I can not take any more pain.
I fear the poking and prodding of my body.
I no longer belong to myself.
My freedom has been taken by them.

My accusers inflict grievance and pain on me.
I see the smiles as they go forward.
I have no champion.
I have no choice.

I hear the cries of cats from my window.
Have they tried and executed them?
Their hate has overflowed to others.
Nothing is safe from their abhorrence.

Life which is so precious is gone.
They have found what they sought.

The sentence will be carried out.
I will burn with my Sisters.

Cries come from other cells.
They have come for all.
Whispers pray to the Goddess for mercy.
They do not hear our prayers.

We are bound to the stake.
Our hands tied behind us.
We no longer whisper.
Our prayers are to the Goddess.

We have come to our end.
Sentenced for our beliefs
Condemned for our practices
Punished for our gifts

I stand tall before them.
We stand together before all.
The flames consume us.
Our light is released.

We have gone where others wait.
Our Sisters wait for us.
Hands comfort our pain.
Love encircles us.

We have gone to the Goddess …

Whispers

In the quiet of the night I hear their whispers.
In the silence of the day I hear their whispers.
As I stand on the balcony I hear their whispers.
Even in a crowd I hear their whispers.
I listen.
I hear their words.
They ask for my prayers.
They ask for my aid.
I hear their words.
I sense their fear.
They stand before me.
I see them.
My hands stretch out for theirs.
I reach for them in the dark.
They stand still.
They come out from the shadows.
Please, know I am here.
I am your Sister.
Come to me and be safe.
Come to me and find comfort.
See the light.
See who I am.
I know you, my Sisters.
Be not afraid.

I release your pain.
I take your terror.
My light surrounds you.
You are released.
The whispers have ceased.
They have found the light.
My Sisters have joined the Goddess.
No more gloom, just light.

All is well...

Victims of Hate

This prayer is dedicated to all the victims of hate.
To those who fight to keep us free.

We gather in our secluded space in the forest.
The wind blows through my hair
Our capes keep us warm against change of season
We stand as the beauty of Mother Earth surrounds us.
A gentle rain falls and we know we are one with the elements

We form our circle around the fire.
We add rosemary, rose petals, cinnamon, and sun flowers to the flames
Each of us comes forward and add incense to the fire
The flames grow.
We feel the power of the Goddess.
Our circle is formed.

Taking the hand of the Sister next to us, we begin.

We bow to the Goddess
We bow to the corners
We bow to each other
We bow to the light
We bow to the power

We feel the animals as they come
We feel those who have passed before us
We feel those who stand with us

Raising our hands we call on the Goddess

We find the love and compassion of the Goddess
We find the love and compassion of each other
We find the love and compassion of the Witches
      from the past
We find the love and compassion of those who
      surround us

We send energy to our families
We send energy to those who live in fear
We send energy to those in pain
We send energy to those in need

We take evil. Fling it into the fire!
We take hate. Fling it into the fire!
We take pain. Fling it into the fire!
We take fear. Fling it into the fire!

We release our power
We release our love
We release our compassion
We release our passion

The animals gather and freely give us their power
The earth sends forth her beauty to us
Those who surround us hold us close
We are safe.

We thank the Goddess
We thank the elements
We thank the animals

We release our hands and know we will be joined soon
As we leave we gather the earth of this space for our work
This space holds our power
We will come again and again
For we are Witches and know our power

Blessed Be

Evil

Evil never wins.
It will always be defeated, but there will be casualties.
I look to the Goddess and see her standing beside me.
I find the power which is mine

I raise my sword and defeat the face of evil with the hands of the Goddess.

She will keep me safe.
For I am her daughter forever.

I gather my Sisters close to me
I gather the strength of the Witches from the past
I gather the animals around me

My prayer begins:

I stand before the Goddess under this full moon. I seize the power of the moon in my hands. I bring the children to my side. The Goddess sends her light to me. My family shows the love that we have for each other. May the Goddess send you her power.

May those around us feel the joy that we bring to the circle. May prosperity fill our lives.

As her daughters we show our love for Mother Earth daily. She shows respect for all that is alive. We pray for those who live in fear to find safety. We pray for those who live in pain to find compassion. We pray for those in cages to run free. See how the birds fly free in our skies. See how the animals roam free. May their days be long.

I send our power to the four corners. I send our wishes to all. Bless the children. Bless our families. Bless the animals. But most ... Blessings to all.

Darkness

As the darkness descends the light remains
For the Goddess will protect her daughter.
Do not fear the dark, for she is there.
Your protection comes from the Goddess.
Your Sisters stand with you.
Be not fearful.
Evil will not prevail.

Stand strong and let her flow through you.

The Darkness Has Come

The darkness has come.
We have gathered.
The circle is formed.
We have called the elements.
The danger is known.
We have drawn down the power.
The danger is near.
We stand strong under the darkness.
The past has come forward.
We are the present.
No danger is greater than us.
We turn and face the enemy,
With arms raised we call forth our Sisters.
A barrier is formed.
From the depth of darkness evil steps forwards.
Protection covers us.
The smell of sulfur fills the air.
A ground swell stands between us.
Stillness
The fight begins
Energy sent for both sides
The ground trembles.
Unnatural sounds can be heard.
Standing firm I step forward.
Hand raised,
Facing evil,
I call on the power of the Goddess.
I am filled with her light and energy.
Light radiates from me in all directions
Striking all that is dark.
They vanish before us.
Evil has been vanquished.
My power fills the emptiness
For we have triumphed over evil.
We remain and always will be.
No power can remove us.
We remain.

Cycles Onward

Dedication

She stands before me.
This maiden
Her linen dress falling gently over her bare feet
A dress stitched with love by her kinfolk
She was brought this night by her sisters
We gather at our Sacred Space
One that belongs to us alone
A space that can be seen by us only.
The forest opens her way to us
Under the moonlight we encircle the maiden
Women of all ages have come this night
Traveling from near and far to be present
Walking with a King's majesty the stag steps forward
He bows in honor to those present.
His bow returned with respect
From the forest a lone wolf steps towards the circle
He takes his place next to the maiden
From this night the stag and wolf belong to her
Sounds from the under bush are heard
The fragrance of heather fills the air
Magick fills the air
The time has come
The maiden will take her place in the sisterhood
I spread my hands and call to the wind
    By Fire
    By Water
    By Earth
    By Air
I call down the moon
I request the Goddess to present her light
Light from the moon shines on the maiden
The women bow towards the light
We are ready.
Each woman takes the hand of her sister next to her
As I step in the center
The skirl of bagpipes are heard by all
We know the lone piper

His song stirs the hearts of those present
The maiden kneels before me
I bless her with oils of frankincense and sandalwood
Herbs placed in the fire rise high
As my words come forth
She has been placed in the arms of the Goddess
The Mother of all has presented herself
Each woman feels her presence
Love fills the circle.
The ground beneath us swells with power
Power rises from the below to encircle all
The air is still except for my words.
Slowly the circle rises from the ground.
The women circle around us as they rise.
The cool earth is felt beneath my feet.
I remain grounded with the maiden.
Flames from the fire reach above our heads,
A gentle rain falls,
The wind encircles us.
Our sisters return to earth
Each is grounded in the light
Quiet returns to our space
The light of the Goddess returns to her
She has left us as each is blessed
We each thank her for her gifts
On the ground lie silver amulets
One for each
As I remove my talisman from its bag
I remember it as my gift from the Goddess
Passing it around the circle each woman
     receives its protection.
As hands drop, the circle opens
Magick and power leave the circle
They fly on the wind to our sisters not present.
The maiden makes her way to each woman
Blessing each sister present
She has now joined the circle
She belongs to the Goddess
And now she belongs to us

I empty the oils on the fire
Embers die
We leave our space
I turn towards our space.
Arms open, I close this space
The forest closes around what is ours
My daughter has taken her place
She soon will take the lead
My time draws near
I long for the Goddess
I long for my husband.
His blue eyes burn in my soul
His touch is gone from me
His voice only remains in my mind

My hands are old and worn.
My power is lessened after this night.
I have freely given it to my daughter.
The stars have fallen.
My sisters leave as I remain.
My stag steps slowly with age towards me
Grey from age my wolf finds me.
I sit beneath the Great Yew.
My time has come.
I feel the heart beat of my wolf,
His coat keeps me warm.
He lays his head in my lap.
I am not alone.
The lone piper plays for me.
Tears drop onto my lap.
My time is near.
My Goddess speaks softly to me:

My daughter give me your hand and follow me.
Close your eyes and become one with the Wind.
Be one with the Rain. Be one with the Earth.
Be one with the power of Fire.
Join your Sisters.

You have always been mine.
You join those who have gone before you.
Be of comfort, all is right this night.
My daughter, join me, for you are loved...

All Will Be Well

He stood so close I could hear his heart beat
I could feel his breath on my back
His strength was felt through my gown
Desire flowed from his soul
I felt warm in his embrace
Our love had endured the ages
The moon rays swirled around us
Heather swayed in the wind
Rain fell gently on our bodies
Fire rose deep within us
I turned and found him
A face that I had known for years
I traced his face with my hands
Each line was known to me
Scars etched deep into his body
I knew each one
His power was well known in our land
My love
From the forest they came
Each standing before him
A low bow in gratitude
Swords and shields held firm
I turned to see our clan
They claimed their leader
They claimed my love
A warrior has risen
I see my future in his eyes
Pain will follow joy
Death will follow life
I carry within me life
For our love will live
Pipes carry the call on the wind
The wolf comes from the shadow
Protection for our clan
The stag walks slowly and releases his authority
A hawk brings forth sight for the unseen
Cunning of the cat is given freely

Gifts for my warrior
Our future has taken form
The Goddess opens the sky
Her light encircles all present
The path has been set
This night our lives will be changed
The warrior goes forth
Turning back we lock eyes
For my power goes with him
I send all that I have to him
My pain felt
The Goddess holds me close
A whisper is heard
My daughter, all will be well

Life

Life flows like a river.
Sometimes the river is calm,
Flowing peacefully.
Then life steps in
It becomes destructive
A force to be tamed
We stand on the shore and see its power
Hitting against the rocks
The water vibrates with sound
It erodes the boulders
Sediment reaches the bed
Nature braces against its power
For the river force, as life, has no boundaries.

Cry

A gentle cry is heard from the room
Life has come forth
Born into this time
A Witch has come
Her Sisters have been called
They bring their gifts
The room is filled with the light of the Goddess
Silver rays flow into the room
The Goddess presents herself
All bow to her grace
In her arms she holds the infant
She breathes the authority of energy
Upon the earth she stands
Power rises towards those present
Slowly the infant rises from her arms
The wind carries her from Sister to Sister
Each one passes their gift to her
The cauldron fires increase
Flames dance in the fire
The flutter of wings is heard
For the Fae have come
They surround all that are present
Rain falls from the sky
The stag has found his way to her
A grey wolf guards the door
In the distance the screech of an eagle
All have come to be present
For the future has come forth
A Witch has been born.

The Night Belongs to Us

As the world sleeps

      We awake

We look towards the moon

      She sends her power

Feeling the wind

      We gather her strength

Our capes flap in the wind

      Wind encircles us

Taking hold of our brooms

      Control comes to us

We ride high this night

      Our silhouettes against the moon

Ride high my Sisters

      The night belongs to us

Hands

I gaze deep into the fire.
The red embers reflect in my eyes.
Holding up my hands over the fire
I turn them over and over.
Lowering them into my lap,
Looking deep into my palms
I trace each line with my index finger.
Slowly tracing those lines, I saw my past.

Were these the hands that slipped into my father's?
The ones that cupped my sister's face when she was born,
That worked the earth with my mother,
Whose grandmother held strong under the Full Moon.

Were these the hands that rose towards the Moon?
That was dedicated to the Goddess.
Whose power was released by my Sisters?
The ones that healed others.

Were these the hands that called the Wind?
That held the earth so Blessed.
Whose power brought the rain?
The ones that fuel the fire.

Were these the hands that held the sword against our foe?
That held the reins of my mount,
Who directed our men?
The ones that felt the death of our enemy.

Were these the hands that joined my love?
That traced his strong and powerful body.
Who felt his passion?
The ones that knew I was loved.

Were these the hands that brought forth life?
That held my children,
Who felt their tender body in my arms?

The ones who cared for and loved her family.

Were these the hands that called forth our ancestors?
That drew down the Full Moon,
Who felt the power of our Sisterhood?
The ones that drew forth the influence of the Goddess.

Were these the hands that held her husband's hand?
That felt the loss of my companion.
Who covered his remains?
The ones that laid him lovingly in the earth.

Yes, these were the hands that had seen the ages,
That had grown old under the Moon,
Who had felt such pain and loss.
The ones that rose high as I long for the Goddess,
That longed for the ones that had gone before me.
Who had remained dedicated to the Goddess.
I feel her slip her hand in mine.
I have left this life to start another,
For we return to continue our journey.
My hands will lead me to another.

For

For

I

Am

Witch

And

Shall

Remain.

Glossary

All That Is – Just that. This is one of many names for Source or Deity in all facets in combination with all that exists.

Fae – A respectful term for the fairy folk. This is one of several correct variations of the spelling.

Magick – This spelling was adopted in order to differentiate religious witchcraft from stage magic and sleight of hand. This was first used in Traditional British Wicca and also by the order of the Golden Dawn.

Phlox – A type of flower mostly found in Northern America, although that is not the only place. There are 67 types of this five petaled flower.

Sgain dubhs – A small single edged Scottish blade traditionally worn by men with their kilts. It is also used in various strains of Wicca and Witchcraft. Some are bone handled and some black handled. This was and is worn tucked into the sock, and on the left or the right depending on which hand is the wearer's dominant hand. Some witches wear theirs on a belt with their ritual garb instead of in their sock. Others also know this as the athame.

Note:
My self vs. Myself and similar – The author and editor have intentionally chosen to differentiate different types of self for different levels, and this is not a typographical error. Myself, themselves, and similar would be the ordinary level. However my self, her self, and similar focus around what creates the self. That then is what is presented in such instances.

About the Poetess

"Our deepest fear is not that we are inadequate. Our deepest fear is that we are powerful beyond measure. It is our light, not our darkness that most frightens us..." Marianne Williamson.

The path that one picks for themselves is bound with barriers. There are times these barriers slow us down. It is then that we must gather our will and power and go forth. I have found this is to embrace my self, to embrace what makes me special. We each have something to offer each other.

I am different. I knew this as a child and grew into it as a woman. It makes me special. It makes me who I am. It is our fear that keeps us in the "Broom Closet." My friends, the closet is filled. Come into the light of the day. Hold on to your broom.

Say it out loud...I am a Witch.

It took me a long time to say those words. Words have their own power. They also can create fear. But I am better for who I am. Let the world know your power. Let them know your knowledge you hold, the knowledge that you have always held. Your mothers and sisters have given this to you. We were the first to look deep into the fire. We were the first to raise our arms towards the moon and praise her glory. We see all. The music comes to us, for the words are deep in our soul.

Walk tall. Hold tight to your broom. All that surrounds you belongs to us. We know the splendor, but also the darkness that is ignorance.

For all those who have died in vain. For all those who have lived in fear. For all those have felt the torment of difference. I stand proud before you and bow to your courage.

Witch, Witch, you're a Witch ... Yes I am!

JoAnne Spiese

Made in United States
Troutdale, OR
10/23/2023